THE CHURCH AFTER THE COUNCIL

THE CHURCH
AFTER THE COUNCIL

Karl Rahner

HERDER AND HERDER

1966
HERDER AND HERDER NEW YORK
232 Madison Avenue, New York 10016

Original editions: "Das Konzil—Ein neuer Beginn," Freiburg, Verlag Herder, 1965; "Das neue Bild der Kirche," Würzburg, Echter-Verlag, 1966 (*Geist und Leben*); "Die Herausforderung der Theologie durch das II. Vatikanische Konzil," Freiburg, Verlag Herder, 1966. Translated by Davis C. Herron and Rodelinde Albrecht.

Library of Congress Catalog Card Number: 66–26676
© 1966 by Herder and Herder, Inc.
Manufactured in the United States

Contents

THE CHURCH AFTER THE COUNCIL

THE COUNCIL
A NEW BEGINNING

CHAPTER ONE

THE Second Vatican Council has ended. Usually when something extraordinary has come to an end, one tries to look back and determine what really happened. History shrouds itself in mystery, and now, at the end of the Council, we pause to evaluate, question, express our gratitude, and to ask, What was it? Where do we stand? What will be accomplished?

1. A Council of the Liturgy and the Missions

What was it? A Council of the holy Roman Catholic Church. Has the Church passed the test which God has given her in this hour? If we say yes, then we affirm our obligation to give God the most heartfelt gratitude for his grace, for any accomplishment is due to God's grace alone.

What was it? A Council! It was that, and that indeed suffices to make it significant. It would be very difficult at this point to predict precisely how or whether the recent proclamation of the collegial-synodal principle of the Church will take concrete form and be put into actual operation. It is impossible to foretell whether the newly founded senate of bishops will be merely consultative or whether it will comprise in theological essence a Council itself by carrying out the mandates of the Second Vatican Council (even though frequent interference and restrictions may hamper it in this task). But that the Council was, that the Church ventured to tackle problems and to come to grips with questions vital to her being, that alone is of inestimable theological significance for the Church's self-understanding in theory and practice. It has demonstrated specifically that the collegial-synodal principle of the Church is not violated in the institution and office of the papacy; and further, the Council has shown that, though this principle has been somewhat deëmphasized in the past it has remained a real power in the Church. The Church has shown by the very fact of the Council that her mysterious unity, a unity of personal and collegial structure subsisting only by the power of God, cannot be measured by the standards or norms of any other existing secular or social organization. The Church is, in truth, a mystery of faith which surmounts all the problems implicit in other structures, whether authoritarian or democratic. Yes, one might even venture to suggest for further consideration the idea that this sort of conciliar system might prove to be meaningful in the secular social-political context as a device for debate and final appeal when the mass society of tomorrow seeks to resolve the conflicting claims of freedom and unity.

It was a Council, a constitutional community which demonstrated and took its own initiative, a Council which was respected by the *primus* of the Church, who as its head according to Catholic understanding worked with it as with the community of his brother bishops, not as a random gathering of "yes-men." This working together of the pope and the Council has never been adequately institutionalized in correct procedural norms, and consequently there were during the Council many hours of darkness and many painful experiences which were almost necessarily unavoidable. It is proved both by history and by experience that the Church never guides herself but is guided, in fact as in theory, by the power of the Spirit—she remains *One* not merely literally, but rather in the incomprehensible plurality of her personal and collegial structure through the miracle of the Spirit.

It was a Council in freedom and in love. The Council, within the freedom of that grace which joined all its members in steadfast devotion to our Lord Jesus Christ, explored the growing understanding in faith of the dogmas of the Church while remaining equally loyal to the already accepted faith of the Church. Truly, it was a Council in freedom, that I can assure you. As a participant in the work behind the scenes, I acknowledge the pomposities, the weaknesses, and the prejudices characteristic of all men, even of men who are doing the work of God. But I can witness to the fact that there was real freedom there within which all sides were honorably occupied in doing those things which pertain to God in the service of love and freedom. If anyone is unable to recognize this fact regarding those who differed with him, he convicts himself of narrow party spirit. Seemingly, human virtues and humility are bestowed by God's good providence equally in all directions, upon the *avant-garde* as upon the opposition. The truly miraculous and astonishing thing about this Council was that genuine unanimity was reached in freedom. Common declarations and common agreement were achieved. It is not just to be assumed that this sort of unanimity can be expected in the present day. One can easily get the impression nowadays that freedom has caused, at least in the field of theology, discord, and that only by the show of authority can one make any appreciable advances in thought or activity. But the Council demonstrated that with the grace of God this is not necessarily so. Naturally, such unity in freedom is achieved only with great effort, and here and there a step on the way may seem at first sight to be merely a bad compromise. But this is actually the way unity in true freedom is realized. Therefore, I would bid the skeptical critics of the Council, both within and without the Catholic Church, to ask themselves, before undertaking to criticize the particulars, where else than in the Catholic Church such unity in the realm of thought and conviction is possible and evident in the present world, especially in the dimension of the Churches and their theologies. Here is a phenomenon of intellectual history which cannot be explained through "ideological" and "sociological" hypotheses of the Church insofar as they are empirically experienced. Here it has turned out that in the Church unity and fidelity to her own historical mission have not frozen into immobility, nor has freedom of thought degenerated into empty rhetoric and idle ramblings.

It was a Roman Catholic Council. The faith of this Church, our faith, was the law and the norm of this Council. If anyone expected anything else—if he thought that *everything* should be questioned, that the appearance of unity should be achieved through irresponsibility, that the dogmas of the past should be surrendered for the cheap, trite, vulgar opinions of Everyman, instead of being allowed their organic development according to their own sense into full universality within our understanding of the faith—then he misunderstood a Council of our Church from the very outset. Should anyone have been disappointed or surprised that the results of the Council did not meet his own expectations, that is no special cause for bewilderment. This Council was in every sense of the word catholic, yet, in a way until recently almost inconceivable, also entirely a Council of ecumenical responsibility. This was not made true simply by the presence of observers from other Christian communities and Churches who played a real role in the proceedings, nor simply because there was a decree on ecumenism, nor because the Council avoided the old controversies and theological pitfalls which lie in the way to the realization of the unity of all Christians, nor because we silenced our own faith and denied our own insights in order to create something new because we believe that no final or permanently valid doctrinal categories are to be found. This ecumenical spirit is manifested not just in the effort to take into account non-Catholic Christians and their theologies in the conciliar expressions as far as it was possible without compromising

15

the Church's own doctrinal convictions, but above all because the Council endeavored in its doctrinal understanding to engage intensively in dialogue with all Christians by expressing more clearly old verities in new ways. The significance of this attitude for an ecumenical theology of the future cannot yet be comprehended. I refer, for example, to the declarations on the collegial principle in the Church, on the significance of the charismatics within the Church, on the local congregation as *Church,* on the salvation of the non-Christian, on the hierarchy of significance among even the defined truths of the faith, on the Scripture which serves the Church and her teaching office, on the general priesthood, on the plurality of equally valid theologies in the one Church, on the personal freedom of belief, on the significance and the rightness of a historical-critical theology, on the falsity of a two-storey theory of a higher and a lower morality and sanctity in the Church, on the meaning of the Service of the Word, and so forth.

The Council was without doubt far and away the most productive of all the Church's ecumenical councils to date. It was a Council which undertook the greatest tasks so far and the most far-reaching themes. Let no one say that this should be entirely assumed since the technical possibilities of today as compared to former times are so much greater. The business had already been basically worked over during the preliminaries to the Council (though in many ways too much so). But when one realizes what preconceptions many people had in those days—especially in Roman circles—of the course of the Council, one can see that it would have been naïve to assume a smooth course. Some participants, for example, believed beforehand that the Council had as its task merely to codify a little more solemnly than before the old dogmatic assumptions, and that the real job could in effect be finished before the opening of the Council. However, it happened otherwise (as we all know now), and it would be a sign of short-sightedness and ingratitude if we looked back on what happened as merely what could have been assumed, and to evaluate everything as having been inevitable. For everything at the Council was reworked from the ground up. Naturally, it was necessary to make a preliminary selection and to impose a thematic limitation on the tasks of the Council, and it need not be denied that we can by hindsight detect here and there a certain fortuitousness in the inclusions or exclusions. But just as no former Council had consisted of this enormous assembly of the entire Church, so no former Council had as its objective the full scope of the task of the Church. One has only to glance at the themes of the Council and to try to arrange them in meaningful order to realize the magnitude of the task undertaken. They are:

1. The fundamental self-understanding of the Church in the *Dogmatic Constitution on the Church, Lumen Gentium.*

2. The inner life of the Church:

Her ministry of sanctification (*munus sanctificandi*), notably the liturgy as expressed in the *Constitution on the Sacred Liturgy.*

Her pastoral ministry (*munus regendi*) in the decree on the episcopate, *De Pastorali Episcoporum Munere in Ecclesia;* and in the decree on the Oriental Catholic Churches.

Her teaching ministry (*munus docendi*), in the *Dogmatic Constitution on Divine Revelation* (with the schema on Scripture, tradition, and the teaching office) and in the *Declaration on Christian Education.*

Her states of life, in the decrees on the priesthood and the service, life, and formation of the clergy; in the decree on the suitable renewal of the religious life; and in the decree on the lay apostolate.

3. The mission of the Church to those outside:

Her relationships with non-Catholic Christendom in the *Decree on Ecumenism* and in the decree on the Oriental Churches.

Her relationships with non-Christians in the declaration on the non-Christian religions, including the Jews, and in the decree on the missionary activity of the Church.

Her relationships with the modern secular world in the *Pastoral Constitution on the Church in the Modern World,* and also in the decree on modern communications.

Her relationships with the pluralism of world-views characteristic of our age, especially in the *Declaration on Religious Freedom.*

When one looks at the themes treated by the Council one can truly say that the Church has done her best to face squarely the problems presented by our age—she has brought together into a real unity problems and formulations emerg-

18

ing contemporaneously in what might seem otherwise to be only a fortuitous juxtaposition. One may not accuse the Church of having turned, introvert fashion, into herself. Certainly, she speaks of herself in all these declarations, but she is considering in all expressions how she can *serve*— God, man, the world, and her destiny. We state, in conclusion, quite clearly and positively, that this Council was the first really all-encompassing ecumenical Church assembly, one which we might well call a Council of the liturgy and a Council of the missions.

2. *The Beginning of the Beginning*

And now, what? Can it be maintained that the Church has consummated her *aggiornamento,* that she has fulfilled the task given her? Can one say that the Church is now youthful and fresh, eager to confront the unknown spiritual adventures lying in the future for a mankind of so great number, a mankind which is highly organized, technologically sophisticated, automated, capable of influencing its own future development, of reaching out to the super-terrestrial realms of outer space which portend so much good and so much deadly terror? It would certainly not be advisable, and in fact one should dare not attempt, to make such a claim. Nothing would be more dangerous than an over-enthusiastic attitude. The Council marked the decisive beginning of the *aggiornamento,* it established the renewal, it called us to the ever necessary repentance and return; in other words, it was only the beginning of the beginning.

If it did all of this, the Council accomplished a great deal; but all that it accomplished was still by way of beginning. Everything, almost everything, that the Council declared is still in the form of written intention. It is all print, out of which can come spirit and life, service, faith, and hope, but print is not the reality which is striven after. The Church has recognized her task, but she has yet to fulfill it. For we must recall that the Church, according to one of our most fundamental insights in fire and the Holy Spirit, is we ourselves. We are the Church.

Beginning of beginning . . . beginning of what? First of all, of course, the beginning of that which was, and is, and ever shall be, Jesus Christ, who is the same yesterday, today, and forever; the beginning of his grace which alone redeems us and opens unto us access to the living God; but beginning of beginning so that Jesus Christ and his Church may truly encounter the spirit of this and the future age.

Therefore, the Council was the beginning of beginnings for the Church of the limitless grace of God; for a Church of our Lord and Saviour; for a Church of the word of God, of brotherhood, of hope, of humble love and service, of joy in the Holy Spirit, a Church of love which conquers all legalisms; for a Church which is able to recognize her own being and to go out to meet the deepest longings and needs of our age, a Church which learns in that she teaches, receives in that she gives, rules in that she serves. The Council was the beginning of the beginning of a Church who already is and always will be what she is, in that she turns anew to her only source, who is both the Beginning and the Lord of history, the Lord who has led and will lead the Church on into the unknown future. And there is much, almost too much that needs to be done in order to initiate this beginning.

We must yet translate the instructions of the *Constitution on the Sacred Liturgy* into concrete forms for the celebration of the liturgy, we must yet transform them into the real prayer-life of the Church, worship in spirit and in truth. Now the ecumenical dialogue must truly begin, patiently, humbly, courageously, optimistically, and audaciously. We do not as yet have the deacons for whom the Council has created new opportunities in the Church. The episcopate has yet to show that it can make real in the Church in a new and living way the unity of the collegial principle of the Church. The promised reforms of the Roman Curia have only begun to be codified and put into practice in real life. It will take many years of hard work before the Canon Law can be made to reflect in spirit and in the letter the reforms of this Council. All the prudent and courageous norms laid down for the formation of the clergy, for priestly activities, for episcopal activities, the norms for the college of bishops, all these things must be actualized and become a living reality in the daily life and habitual operations of the Church. The religious life is not yet renewed merely because there has been a decree concerning it. The laity, endued with the universal priesthood, have not become fully responsible and aware of their apostolic mission simply because the documents of the Council edifyingly—I use the word in its best scriptural sense—used such a term. Holy Scripture has not been enshrined in the hearts of men and become central in the parochial liturgy as the Word of Life simply because each day at the Council the Gospel book was enthroned with ceremony and because, in addition to the many allusions praising Scripture, there was approved a constitution which lauded the meaning of Scripture for the life of the Church. The decree on the missions is not yet identical with the missionary will. This shall be the missionary spirit of the Church in practical everyday life, in actual practice, when, for example, bishops will send to the missions priests whom they sorely need, when money is given which could also be prudently used at home. A board of directors for ecumenical work has yet to be established. The statutes for the national conferences of bishops have yet to be drawn up and ratified. The decree concerning the formation of future priests has yet to be dealt with by the regional episcopal conferences, and many other matters referred by the Council to the regional episcopal conferences are yet to be accomplished. The work on the Canon Law of the Eastern Churches which began under Pius XII must now be carried out in the light of the new paths opened by this Council. Difficult individual problems which were taken under consideration and which in their complexity and urgency have become in some sense a measure of the success of the Council—such problems as the laws regulating mixed marriages, marital relations, penance, and indulgences—still remain unsettled.

The newly founded secretariats for non-Christians and non-believers must yet prove themselves not to be still more bureaucratic, hypertrophied appendixes operating according to Parkinson's Law. The Oriental Catholic Churches must yet demonstrate that they have the will and the power to undertake their own missionary activity, and the Latin Church must still demonstrate that she regards these Churches as more than honorable museum pieces preserved as relics of the past. The Church must also learn how to protect freedom, must learn to walk humbly and modestly with her organized social power, to be more noble, more open, more patient, more tolerant, even as she is with herself. The Church must now engage in dialogue with the world in all its needs, possibilities, and dangers, a dialogue which she has undertaken and outlined in the far-reaching pastoral constitution on the Church's relationship to the modern world. She should, she must state frankly that this or that point in the conciliar work, besides being the work of the Holy Spirit, remains also the work of men, imperfectly done, and only begun, reflecting better the past than the future. This is true especially of the decree on communications and the declaration on Christian education. It still remains to be seen how the fundamental and ambitiously conceived instruction on the now permissible *"communicatio in sacris"* can be practically, despite the necessary limitations, worked out and put into practice. The conversation with contemporary athe-

23

ism and the need for faith characteristic of our day, which the *Pastoral Constitution on the Church in the Modern World* has declared to be necessary, must now be carried through into reality. The magnificent conception that each diocese must help the others in realistic deeds must yet be actualized so that the idea does not become simply a pious gesture which costs one diocese little trouble and is as of little help to the other. These things and many others remain to be done. This is a task which the Council has not completed, but which it has laid upon the Church because she is commissioned by God.

Above all, a new theology must be found which is worthy of Vatican II and of the task assigned to the Church. It is not as though the theology of today were not good, but because it can become better, because it must delve ever deeper into the depths of the knowledge of God and deal more radically with the questions that the future holds out for us, for theology must be able to serve the proclamation of the Church of tomorrow. One task which certainly should be undertaken immediately is a thorough thinking through of the texts of the Council, an exhaustive commentary on them; further, these documents need to be put in full historical perspective. This would be excellent; this must be done at all costs. But the post-Vatican II theology would not be worthy of the Council if it accomplished this and only this as its chief task. There are many other questions which present themselves, questions which would not have been inappropriate and could have been themes of the Council, the old

24

questions, which always remain pertinent and always present themselves in epochal new ways: how theology can speak of God, and his existence in the midst of mankind, in such a way that the words can be understood by the men of today and tomorrow; how it can so proclaim Christ in the midst of an evolving universe that the word of the God-man and the incarnation of the eternal Logos in Jesus of Nazareth do not sound like myths which men cannot any longer take seriously; how it can relate human ideologies and plans for the future with the Christian eschatology; how it can assure humanity that in the *eschaton* redemption has already been achieved, so that men do not relapse into the position of the men of the old covenant who dreaded death as though it meant separation from the God of life; how it can show that love of God and love of neighbor always form in a new and epochal way an absolute unity, love which one without the other is incomprehensible and unattainable, especially since God is manifested for us through Christ in mankind and thus is for us only so attainable; how and why the cross will always loom over the realm of human existence and why, even in the triumphal future, mankind will always be nailed to the cross and that only through death and patient seeking through the darkness of existence will men find the entrance into eternal life. These and similar eternal, old, ever radically new, never-solved questions will be the questions for the theology of tomorrow which will be worthy of the Council. When, and I maintain only when, the theologians of all Christian confessions restate these questions anew in common language and not in the language of the old polemical theology, then will they come nearer to each other and put into operation a truly ecumenical theology.

The Council has undertaken tasks and dealt with themes which, measured by the concrete realities which face the Church for the moment, doubtless could not have been more ambitious. However, measured by the challenges which face the Church in the coming decades, these topics represent only a beginning, a remote preparation and a preliminary fitting-out for the pressing tasks of the future. For this future does not ask the Church for the precise details of our ecclesiology, nor for a more exact and lovelier ordering of the liturgy, nor for more precise distinctions in controversy with the theologies of non-Catholic Christians, nor for a more or less ideal regulation of the Roman bureaucracy, but, rather, whether the Church can so faithfully testify to the redeeming and fulfilling presence of that ineffable mystery whom we call God that the men of the age of technology, who have already made so many advances towards control of their world and destiny, can experience the power of this unspeakable mystery in their lives. The Church will be asked with hitherto unparalleled severity—to return again to an old theme for our example—whether she can so comprehend and express the mystery of the God-man that this fundamental dogma of Christendom does not appear to be some merely archaic, correct, lifeless, and dead formula, but to be that blessed incomprehensibility in terms of which all other things are for the first time understandable, as the divine authentication of man himself who discovers for the first time that his existence in the eternity of his freedom means the possibility of activity and not just of contemplation, that it is a promise that even death, guilt, and all the absurdity which governs mankind and seems to grow and not diminish with his history, is surrounded and swallowed up by the light and salvation of God. The Church will be asked more inexorably by the future than heretofore whether her love of mankind on account of the love of God is stronger and more victorious than the love that links man to man within the dungeon of his own existence without showing him the way across the infinite abyss of the divine.

Such themes could not be the immediate tasks of this Council, perhaps could not be the objectives of any Council. However, they will confront the Church of the future because they have always been and always will be the most authentic themes of Christianity. Therefore, all the answers and solutions of the Second Vatican Council are not capable of being more than a beginning of the mission of the Church to the future just breaking upon us. Seen thusly, the efforts and results of the Council seem not unimportant, but rather to achieve their undeniable significance.

The *aggiornamento* which the Church has undertaken is not an effort to make the Church more attractive to and comfortable for the world, but chiefly to prepare the Church in advance to deal with the questions of life and death which will confront her. And from this perspective also, the Council is only a beginning.

It is necessary to add a word of warning: it would be a fearful error and a terrible delusion of the heart, but it is a real danger (from which, we may believe, not even the indestructible Church has been protected from the first), should one think that after the Council one can simply go on with everything just as it was before because what was said, decided, and taught at the Council was either already assumed in practice or dealt with only peripheral and unimportant things or consisted only of pious ideals which one sets down on the ever-indulgent paper for one's own self-edification. Naturally, the Church must always be true to her own nature and traditions, rightly understood. Things won't be better tomorrow. The holy Church will always remain, even in the future, the Church of poor sinners, for we are all the *ecclesia semper reformanda in capite et in membris,* the Church always needing reform in head and in members.

It will certainly be a long time before the Church which has been given the Second Vatican Council will be the Church of the Second Vatican Council, just as it took a number of generations after the close of the Council of Trent before she became the Church of the Reform of Trent. But this does not alter in the least our own terrible responsibility, which we all who are in the Church have been invited to fulfill: to do what we have said we will do, to become that which we have recognized ourselves to be and before all the world have acknowledged ourselves to be, to make deeds out of words, to make spirit out of rules, to make true prayer out of liturgical forms, and reality out of ideas. The Council could hardly be more than the beginning of this task, but that is a great deal, and it is more than one can express in mere words.

It would be a difficult judgment indeed, both for sheep and shepherd, for us all, if we should confuse word and deed, beginning and fulfillment. We have in the Council, just as Elijah did of old, wandered through the desert and have come nearer to God upon the holy mountain. If we would like to stretch out, tired and sleepy, under the broom tree of a conciliar triumphalism, then an angel of God may, yea he must, by means of the frightful dangers and anxieties of our time, by means of persecution, apostasy, and pain of heart and spirit, wake us up out of our sleep: Rise up, a long road lies ahead of you (see 1 Kings 19, 7).

3. *Towards the Future*

I know that the clever and skeptical will criticize these statements as being only pretty words by which we seek to soothe the incurable chronic misery of existence and to talk away the doubts of the Church. Certainly, it would be foolish and naïve to maintain that the Church will suddenly cease to be the tired pilgrim in time, the Church of sinners, of the weak and the wretched, and change suddenly into the bride without spot or wrinkle, visible in all her glory to the eyes of the unbeliever. All renewal, all progress of the Church will at the same time be expended in the experience of the toilsomeness of history, in the disappointment with ourselves who are still the Church. We always intend to play the unfinished symphony of the honor of God, but what we achieve is merely a dress rehearsal. But this does not mean that all effort, all never-finished and never-perfectible reformation is in vain. It is simply the job of the laborer who sows in tears that God may reap, the task which only Christian hope conquers in spite of all hope because it alone knows that all our defeats are assumed and the victory of God is proclaimed on the wood of the cross. Finally, and this is perhaps the last and most important point, everything churchly, therefore everything institutional, legal, sacramental, every word, every occupation in the Church and therefore every reform of all these ecclesiastical affairs, is in the last intention, in the last understanding, if correctly understood and not itself made an idol (if, in other words, not merely considered a means for achieving something else), something entirely simple and so difficult and blessed at the same time: faith, hope, and love in the hearts of all men. To use a secular example, to achieve these things is like extracting radium from pitchblend. One must refine a ton of ore to recover 0.14 gram of radium, yet it is profitable. Every churchly activity, preaching, ruling, theologizing, reforming, every educational effort and every assertion of herself within society, is, with all the attendant enormous investment in plants, equipment, and labor, only somewhat like the mining of an enormous quantity of pitchblend so that in our hearts, and there alone, there can be extracted a tiny bit of the radium of faith, hope, and charity. Thus the Council and all the post-conciliar work so enormously necessary are only service and preparation. This service has as its goal not the self-assertion of the Church in the future, but the arrival of the kingdom of God, the true immortality of man, simply faith, hope, and charity. This artless and eternal goal, which has from the beginning of history lived in the heart of man, which recapitulates the sense of all history and of eternity and the content of its affairs, this is all that happened at the Council, and whatever contradicts this is entirely secondary. Every subtle theology, every dogma, every Church law, every accommodation and denial of the Church, every institution, every bureau and all its powers, every holy liturgy and every brave mission has as its only goal: faith, hope, and love towards God and man. All other plans and deeds of the Church would be absurd and perverse were she to abandon this commission and seek only herself. The Council seeks the heart, which believing, hoping, and loving abandons itself and surrenders itself to the mystery of God. Otherwise it would be a horrible theatrical parody, and the self-idolatry of either man or the Church. These words must be engraved over the Council: "So faith, hope, love abide, these three; but the greatest of these is love" (1 Cor. 13, 13).

The grace of God has given us these achievements of the Council, and now the post-conciliar reforms have been left in our hands as commissions which can be realistically fulfilled. When the government of the bishops is service, humble, humbler than before; when the priests more selflessly and purely, whether with results or not, administer the word of God and the grace of the sacraments; when the laymen criticize less and coöperate more eagerly; when all take up the cross of their existence and carry it after Christ more patiently, and see the light of God in the darkness with brighter eyes of faith; when everyone recognizes himself as a sinner and yet redeemed by the grace of God; when everyone begins to love God more; when everyone tries a little bit more each day to replace the egotistic hardness of his heart with a little more active love of neighbor; when there are Christians who are influenced neither by the brutal bellowing uproar nor by the cowardly whispering of nationalistic or militaristic egotism; when a few Christian men and women in the openness of their living more clearly demand and more clearly say what is right and not what is merely expedient, then the Council will have achieved its goal, will have fulfilled its meaning. This goal disappears into the silent mystery of God, who alone knows our hearts and deeds. But the Church must have the courage to face the inevitability of her mission. Otherwise she would not be what she is and must daily become.

Was it necessary to have a Council for this goal? It *was* necessary, certainly, for even the mystery of human existence, that silently proceeds into the darkness of the eternal light, should and must take place in the brotherly fellowship of the Church. In her, every one must speak with the other, must say everything to all, hear God's word, look at the cross, receive the body of the Lord which was given for all

32

men; must go and become a Christian, a believer, a hoper, a lover.

If the Church in the next decades were to better governed, the liturgy more beautifully celebrated, if more meaningful theology and more open justice and greater Church influence in society were to be achieved, but not more faith, hope, and love, then everything would be in vain. One would have heaped up loads of pitchblend and yet not have extracted any radium. It is up to us, each one of us, each of us in the ordinariness of our lives and in the last single decision of conscience, to accomplish the meaning of the Council in the royal freedom of the children of God. God grant us the grace to accomplish it.

THE CHURCH
A NEW IMAGE

CHAPTER TWO

THE Second Vatican Council, we find if we carefully review all sixteen of its constitutions, decrees, and declarations, was concerned mainly with the Church.

The *Dogmatic Constitution on the Church* and the *Decree on the Church's Missionary Activity* treat of the Church's basic understanding of her nature and destiny.

The Church's teaching office is discussed in the same *Dogmatic Constitution on the Church,* as well as in the *Dogmatic Constitution on Divine Revelation* and the *Declaration on Christian Education.*

The Church's task of sanctifying through the celebration of the sacraments is taken up in the *Constitution on the Sacred Liturgy.*

The government of the Church is examined in the *Decree on the Bishops' Pastoral Office in the Church.*

The various states of life in the Church are reviewed in the *Decree on Priestly Formation,* in the *Decree on the Appropriate Renewal of the Religious Life,* in the *Decree on the Apostolate of the Laity,* and lastly in the *Decree on the Ministry and Life of Priests.*

The relationship of the Catholic Church to other Christian Churches and communities is treated in the *Decree on Ecumenism* and the *Decree on Eastern Catholic Churches.*

The problem of the Church's relationship to non-Christian religions is probed in the *Declaration on the Relationship of the Church to Non-Christian Religions.*

The Church's relevance and role in the modern world is examined in the *Pastoral Constitution on the Church in the Modern World* and in the *Decree on the Instruments of Social Communications.*

Finally, the Church considers her situation in pluralistic society in the *Declaration on Religious Freedom.*

1. A Church Reflecting on Her Nature

The Second Vatican Council, therefore, was a Council of the Church *about* the Church. It was a Council concerned with ecclesiology, the formal study of the Church—with a unity of theme that no previous Council ever had. Even the First Vatican Council, which defined the primacy of papal authority, treated completely unrelated matters along with this question. When we say that the Second Vatican Council was an ecclesiological Council, therefore, a Council concerned with the formal study of the Church, we are not by any means stretching a point. Nor are we overlooking the fact that in addition the Second Vatican Council treated a great number of other truths—and in fact, truths which, in the hierarchy of truths, are more important in themselves than in their direct relationship to the Church. This does not alter the fact, however, that in this Council the Church was not

38

only the subject, but also the object, of the conciliar pronouncements. It does not alter the fact that the Second Vatican Council was a Council of the Church reflecting on her very nature.

At first, such a statement sounds harmless of itself; but if we consider the terrifying, threatening, unknown future facing the Church, we pause in alarm, we ask ourselves in dismay whether the Church has nothing more important to speak about than how she understands herself: for she exists not for herself, but for God, for her Lord, for mankind and its destiny. We could facilely answer this question, of course, by saying that the Church speaks about all these fundamental realities and truths when she speaks about herself. We could say, too, that the Church had to speak about herself because the First Vatican Council had initiated this self-reflexion in its own *Dogmatic Constitution on the Church of Christ,* and that the abrupt suspension of that Council because of the outbreak of the Franco-Prussian War left this self-reflexion incomplete. Or we could say that because ecclesiology has now suddenly become one of the most vital questions, if not the primary question, among Christian Churches everywhere and among their theologians, it was only sensible, indeed requisite, that the Catholic Church partake in this ecclesiological dialogue.

By way of objecting to the first answer, furthermore, one could inquire why the Church feels she must consider the fundamental realities about God, Church, and man in an ecclesiological way, when surely one must now speak with a

39

new tongue about God and his Christ, about man and his future. And regarding the second answer, one might express doubt whether the Council was necessarily acting with initiative and foresight in taking up ecclesiology simply because it is the favorite of modern theology.

These questions, then, their answers, and the objections to the answers are very alarming, but also very important; and in the final analysis, their resolution can only be had along the following lines. In the first place, man, historical man, in view of the manner in which he considers himself both as an individual and as a part of the cosmos, is always in the end the "ultimate problem"; that is, no problem is finally solved, no perspective ensured of its place, until the problem of man is resolved. The same is true of the Church. In any dialogue or discourse, the Church must always consider herself the first and last problem. The very obviousness with which ecclesiology became almost automatically the key theme of the Council shows, therefore, how much man and the Church, with all their ability of reflexion and all their responsibilities towards others, uncannily consider themselves to be the ultimate problem. And this is both a fear and a consolation. It is a fear, because we ask ourselves whether man and the Church are not acting too self-reliantly; and it is a consolation, for we believe that ultimately we find our direction from God.

In the second place, all inquiry into one's self opens out into the future. And the Church's life of faith is still in progress. This means that what she says today, if said truthfully, can perhaps in the unknown tomorrow be said again in a different way, for tomorrow the Church will have greater age, greater maturity, new perspectives, new circumstances. What she says about herself today implies also a recognition of what she intends to be tomorrow.

The final question, therefore, is: How, in her life of faith, can the Church best realize all that she said about herself at the Council?

To be sure, a genuine truth may also miss its *kairos*.* This is certainly true, as we all may know from our own experience, especially of the individual person; but could it not also be true of the experience of the Church? For how otherwise could the Catholic Church, *before* defining a dogma, and apart from her concern for the truth, also inquire after the "opportuneness" of defining that dogma—and thereby imply that the truth of a matter is not the only qualification for its becoming known as definitively true?

As long as history endures, therefore, a truth which has been spoken will endure . . . only for so long as it is incommensurate with the real task of the hour; and that task

---

* Father Rahner has elsewhere defined "*kairos*" as follows: "In Greek philosophy, the term for a period of crisis within a temporal existence at which the person concerned is summoned to historical decision. The *kairos* in Scripture is the time of salvation which God has chosen and decreed (Mk. 1, 15), the fullness of time (Gal. 4, 4), the final offer of God's grace in Jesus Christ to Israel (Lk. 19, 44) and to all men (2 Cor. 6, 2), and therefore simultaneously a final warning, the beginning of the Judgment (1 Pet. 4, 17; Col. 4, 5). *Kairos,* like the biblical 'now,' expresses God's sovereign dominion even over time." *Theological Dictionary,* by Karl Rahner and Herbert Vorgrimler, New York, Herder and Herder, 1965, p. 249 (—Tr.).

will be carried out only with the help of God's grace in us, as we carry this truth patiently into the future, until it finds its moment of grace, which now becomes *our* salvation. And this is what will justify that earlier day when, perhaps too prematurely, perhaps too late, perhaps a bit too rashly or a bit too cautiously, that particular truth came to be recognized —when, like the apple, it was plucked at not quite the right time from the tree of knowledge of good and evil.

We do not intend to assert or insinuate, however, that this was the case with the Church when she chose the theme of ecclesiology at the Second Vatican Council. For how, *today,* could one even be justified in saying such a thing? But on the other hand it is good to have the problem pointed out, for it admonishes us to moderation.

So many things, then, were said at the Council about the Church—things old and new, important and trivial, dogmatic, merely juridical, pastoral, theological—that it is impossible offhand to summarize it all in the brief scope of this chapter. For this reason, therefore, but also because we must begin now (for it is an imperative task) to prepare to recognize when the time of the Church's *kairos* will arrive, we will inquire after only the more important new features which the Church has prescribed for herself—features of her future image—so that she may become that which she already is.

Before we continue, however, we would like to emphasize an important point, namely, that the word "new" as we are using it does not necessarily denote that a truth is being said for the first time. For it would be difficult to determine what might be called "new" in the conciliar ecclesiology in that sense. This is very evident in the fact that the conciliar statement on the synodal collegiality of the episcopacy (and this was perhaps the most controversial theme taken up by the Council) actually only preserves a statement which the Fathers of Vatican I not only did not controvert, but which they explicitly declared was self-evident.

It is perfectly clear: when a Council abandons, rejects as false or inadequate, a teaching which existed in the Church but in an undefined way, there can be no question in this case of progress from the implicit to the explicit. (And such cases are, of course, possible.) But on the other hand, if we adhere to the idea that no new revelation is contained in the Church, but rather that she keeps alive and interprets *one* Christian and apostolic revelation, then we can only conclude that a new *positive* statement on revelation *must* have been present—at least implicitly—in the earlier awareness of faith.

It cannot be the theologian's task, therefore, merely to praise the newness of a discovery in the Council or in theology, as though something plainly new had been found.

But all this means that the word "new" has a double meaning, though at the same time a "unified" double meaning—and *this* is a very important discovery. A truth can be new and vital in the life of the Church, and yet it can be a truth about the Church which in the future will become particularly new and effective.

2. The Presence of the Church in the Local Community

The first feature of the new image of the Church which we must take up regards the Church insofar as she is present in the concrete local community and the community of the altar. A singular text must be referred to here, which appears in Article 26 of the *Dogmatic Constitution of the Church*. That Article reads in part:

"A bishop marked with the fullness of the sacrament of orders is 'the steward of the grace of the supreme priesthood,' especially in the Eucharist, which he offers or causes to be offered, and by which the Church continually lives and grows. *This Church of Christ is truly present in all legitimate local congregations of the faithful which, united with their pastors, are themselves called Churches in the New Testament. For in their locality these are the new people called by God, in the Holy Spirit and in much fullness. In them the faithful are gathered together by the preaching of the Gospel of Christ, and the mystery of the Lord's Supper is celebrated, 'that by the food and blood of the Lord's body the whole brotherhood may be joined together.'* In any community of the altar, under the sacred ministry of the bishop, there is exhibited a symbol of that charity and 'unity of the mystical body, without which there can be no salvation.' In these communities, though frequently small and poor, or living in the diaspora, Christ is present, and in virtue of his presence there is brought together one, holy, catholic, and apostolic Church. For 'the partaking of the body and blood of Christ does nothing other than transform us into that which we consume.'

"Every legitimate celebration of the Eucharist is regulated by the bishop, to whom is committed the office of offering the worship of Christian religion to the divine majesty and of administering it in accordance with the Lord's commandments and the Church's law, *as further defined by his particular judgment for his diocese.* . . ."

Now, does it not seem that the words which we have italicized are out of place, out of context, almost awkwardly pasted in? The answer, of course, is yes.

But let us go back for a moment. It is true that the whole of the *Dogmatic Constitution on the Church* sees the Church first of all as a universal Church, as a world Church, as the unity of all the faithful within the papal-episcopal union. And this is not to imply that considerably more could not be said about the universal Church than merely some remarks about her sociological-juridical structure (as exemplified, more or less, in the ecclesiology of Bellarmine)—and, in fact, the *Constitution,* particularly in Chapters 1 and 2, says much more. For these chapters speak of the unity of the universal Church founded in the mystery of the divine Trinity; of the holy people of God; of the body of Christ in which all of the faithful partake of the one priesthood of Christ, in which each man finds his own gift of grace and his mission, in which each man is called to be a witness to the grace of God.

Even so, however, the *Constitution* does *not* define the

Church from the point of view of the concrete local community and the community of the altar. We will not here go into all the theological, historical, and situational reasons why the Church can be considered from this point of view, but we will say that they are legitimate and in fact necessary. (It must be emphasized from the first, however, that an explicit teaching of the Church—even in Council—is immediately and eminently obligatory first of all in itself, and only secondly in the perspective of why and how it was said.) Therefore, the basic conception of the Church as the universal Church is certainly legitimate, and it is not to be disregarded as unimportant or irrelevant. But there is *another* perspective of the Church contained in the *Constitution* (if only in that out-of-context way which we quoted above), and that is the perspective which sees the Church primarily from the point of view of the local community.

Again, it is not our task here to illustrate the history of our italicized insertion. It can be easily seen that it was inserted into the main text at a relatively late date, into a text which, on the whole, had been based on Catholic Scholastic theology and canonistics, into a text whose general orientation was to see the Church as the universal Church, into a text whose citations of the New Testament can all be considered *a priori*. With regard to the genesis of the text, all that needs to be said here is that it was the wish—though not the exclusive wish, no doubt—of such Council Fathers as Metropolitan Zoghby and Suffragan Bishop Shick that such a statement be made. The final aim of such a wish was very likely inspired not so much by dogmatic or biblical-theological reasons, as by the immediately practical situation: these and other Council Fathers wanted to see the concrete Church of everyday life there, where she celebrates the death of the Lord, breaks the bread of the Word of God, prays, loves, and bears the cross of existence, where reality is truly unequivocal; where it is tangibly more than an abstract theology, or a dogmatic thesis, or some social megalo-organization. It was feared by these Council Fathers that *this* Church would not become clear enough, even if, in present discussions about the Church, one is no longer confined in his topics to the role of the pope and the bishops.

In any case, the insertion was accepted by the Council Fathers readily and gladly. There were no serious debates on or arguments against the added text either among the members of the theological commission entrusted with drafting the *Constitution,* or within the plenum of the Council. But it was not possible, on the other hand—either technically or from the point of view that such a venture might succeed— to restructure the entire *Constitution* from this perspective. And it was therefore for this reason, as Msgr. Philips, the secretary of the theological commission, personally re-affirmed to me afterwards, that a passage was sought into which this point of view could most readily be inserted. Whether or not the choice of passage was the most fortunate one is not the issue. What is important is that the insertion exists, and that it says what was to be said.

With regard to the local community itself, the *Constitu-*

tion gives us a most sublime statement (and it can refer ultimately to the universal Church), namely, that in this community Christ himself, his Gospel, his love, and the communion of the faithful are present. The *Constitution* recognizes and explicitly states the fact that the local community and the community of the altar are not merely administrated dioceses of some religious megalo-organization called the Church. Rather, they are the concreteness of the Church, her loftiest perfection, the presence of Christ—in word and Eucharist and (and this word may not always be used with the desired clarity even in Protestant theology) in love— which unite those who hear the word and who celebrate the supper of the Lord.

It was certainly not to be expected that something would be said in this context about *how* word, Eucharist, and love interact to form the concrete actuality of the Church as the presence of Christ. But it becomes clear in any case that the concept of the Church as the "perfect society" is insufficient as the basic schema for a theological understanding of the Church. For the Church is more than a perfect society—and this not only because, within the framework of the social condition of the Church as a whole, spirit, divine truth, and love are given and continually occur anew. Moreover, it is within the very dimension of sociality itself that the concept of the Church as "perfect society" is shattered, for the whole Church becomes fully present and perfected only in its parts —that is, on the level where the word is proclaimed and the

Eucharist celebrated in love. And this level, the sacramental, is precisely the societal.

In this connection, the *Constitution* returns to the semantic usage of the Acts of the Apostles and of St. Paul's letters: the community at Ephesus, for example, is *the* Church, and not just *a* Church (the plural word "Churches" used in our italicized insertion having no real weight in view of the preceding "This Church of Christ is truly present in all legitimate local congregations . . ."). In view of this approbation by the *Constitution*, therefore, we too may take up, and in fact we are exhorted to take up, contemplation of this ecclesiology of the local Church, and to let it become living and real for us.

Certainly, such an ecclesiology is far from being thought out fully. We do know, however, that the Church of the future will be characterized by the marks of the local community: poverty, few in number, diaspora. In other words, the future ecclesial experience is anticipated already by the ecclesial experience of the local community. For the man of the future will encounter the Church of the future only when he sees in the Church the presence of Christ realized and experienced in the legitimate kerygma of the Gospel and in the anamnesis of Christ's death in the Eucharist. This is where the Christian of tomorrow will apprehend the actual nature of the Church, for this is where the most original religious and theological experience of the Church will take place: in the local community.

It follows, therefore, that such a community, aware of itself as an ongoing event in the Church in word and sacrament, will know itself to be united with all other communities, who will share their identity with the Church. In accordance with the will of Christ, the local community will allow and endeavor to see achieved this pneumatic communion and unity become concrete in the social sphere as well; and it will understand this to be a great obligation. In faith the community will comprehend that it preserves the truth of the word and its effectiveness in actualizing Christ by no other means than by being part of the hierarchically structured unity of the communities of Christ. It will thus recognize and live whatever the *Constitution* says of the universal Church as such—though it will recognize and live all this, to be sure, as the *Decree on Ecumenism* says, "remembering that in Catholic doctrine there exists an order or 'hierarchy' of truths, since they vary in their relation to the foundation of the Christian faith" (Art. 11).

But the only really important thing is this: that the experience and actuality of Christ, crucified and risen, who by his saving word penetrated into the incomprehensibility of God, is made present in the local community gathered round the altar, so that the Church is thus ever occurring anew in the midst of the paltry wretchedness and perdition of a community of believers, in the vast wilderness of their existence. All other understanding of the Church will live, will be able to live, only on this basis. Whatever the Christian encounters in his community from now on, he will no longer experience as something which happened in the Church, but as an occurrence *of the Church.*

3. The Church as the Sacrament of the World's Salvation

As we study this new feature of the image of the Church, considered in its future historical-situational significance, we suddenly discover the theological and existential locus for yet another "new" thought in conciliar ecclesiology; and it is a thought, moreover, which is frequently in danger of being lost in an ecclesiology which appears to concern itself primarily with the external structure of the Church. It is this: that the *Constitution* calls the Church the *sacramentum* of the world's salvation (Arts. 1, 9, and 48).

To see why an understanding of the Church as the sacrament of the world's salvation is so important for today and tomorrow, we must first examine in this conciliar text a dialectical statement in which two apparent antitheses are forcibly brought together. On the one hand, the *Constitution* says that every man who acts in sincere accord with his conscience attains the salvation of God in Christ, whether he be Catholic, non-Catholic Christian, non-Christian, or agnostic (Art. 16). On the other hand, it is said that the Church of Christ—which *subsists* in the Roman Catholic Church—is necessary for salvation (Art. 14), and that she is destined for all men, and all men are destined for her.

A further difficulty arises when we look at the *Decree on*

the Church's Missionary Activity, at the *Pastoral Constitution on the Church in the Modern World,* at the *Decree on Ecumenism,* the *Decree on the Eastern Catholic Churches,* the *Declaration on Religious Freedom,* and at the *Declaration on the Relationship of the Church to Non-Christian Religions.* For in the promulgation of these documents the Council certainly did not expect the Church to become, within any predictable length of time, effectively and in social actuality, *the* Church to *all* men. Rather, the Council was aware that the Church remains in diaspora, in a pluralistic society, and that in all probability she will become even more so the Church in diaspora. Only by means of this realization, by way of the dialectical antithesis which we have just seen, will the theological and existential situation of the Church as sacrament of the world's salvation become clear to us; only by this means will we attain that Church-consciousness which must be recognized and lived today and tomorrow.

The Christian, then, must come to know the Church as the sole sanctifier, for he will not find in this world any church which is in historical, social actuality the church of all, or which will become the church of all within the foreseeable future. But on the other hand, he cannot, he may not have as his own that idea of the early Christians that all the members of the Church are those who, by and large, have been called out of the *massa damnata* of the rest of mankind and unto salvation. Nor may he subscribe to an ecclesiological relativism (also tacitly accepted by many Catholic Christians), the theory that in the last analysis it does not really matter which Church one belongs to, so long as one faithfully abides by the precepts of that Church which he finds most agreeable.

In this connection, moreover, it is not particularly helpful for the Christian to see his baptism and his Christianity (meaning his orthodox, institutional religion) as the "ordinary" or "regular" way to salvation, while the salvation of the countless others happens to be accomplished in an "extraordinary way," in a way "not according to the rules." For if sheer quantity has anything to do with it, as the Christian will soon come to see, these so-called exceptions therefore actually constitute the norm.

If Christianity, then, *is* Christ, the absolute action of God for man, in which God gives his very self, then Christianity —the Church—cannot renounce its claim to absolute character and universal mission. But on the other hand, the Church and the Christian may not see this claim to be binding on the Church (other than as a purely ideological postulate) only in some unpredictably far-away future. Rather, the Church and the Christian must recognize that the Church *as salvific reality* (and not only as a benevolent and experienced partner in dialogue) *now* has an actual and positive relationship to the non-ecclesial world.

This is what is meant when we say that the Church is the sacrament of the world's salvation, and this is also the mean between the two dialectical statements contained in the *Constitution*. Taken earnestly, the word describing the Church

53

as the sacrament of the world's salvation means this: that the Church is the concrete historical *appearance* in the dimension of history become eschatological, in the dimension of society, for the unique salvation which occurs, through God's grace, across the length and breadth of mankind.

The Church is related to the world's salvation in a way analogous to the way in which the sacramental word and grace are related to the salvation history of the individual. Grace and sacrament have an inner cohesion, but they are not identical; they can precede one another in the temporal order of history; grace may already be given where the sacrament is not yet given; a valid sacrament may yet need to find fulfillment in that very grace which the sacrament signifies. Similarly, the Church is the authentic historical appearance of grace which *everywhere* offers itself as salvation; and although it is present and corroborated in sacramental-historical actuality and in the reflexiveness of the categorical preaching of the Gospel, it does not occur only where this explicitness, this social visibility, this verbalized reflexiveness makes itself fully present, that is, ecclesially, thereby once more realizing a portion of the Church as the historical actuality of itself.

For this very reason, however, the *ecclesial,* objectifying appearance of a grace is at the same time the *appearance of* and *reference to* this grace *itself,* wherever it may occur; it is a sacramental sign of the grace offered to all the world and history. The world, humanity, and human history certainly cannot be Christianly viewed as merely the sum total of individuals concerned with their own salvation and their own private salvation history. If such were indeed the case, then instead of the incarnation of the Logos in the unity of race, there would have had to appear a purely spiritual word of God speaking to the depths of each individual's own consciousness, and salvation history would have to be interpreted in a purely existential way. But the original-sacramental and the basic-sacramental words of salvation within this unity of mankind which embraces the individual and his history are, respectively, Christ, and the historical permanence of his existence, the Church. The basic-sacramental word of grace to the world does indeed operate in the individual; in fact, it is to become actual, individually and sacramentally, in the expressed word and in the substantial sacrament, just as this same basic-sacramental word of grace is established for the world through the community of those who receive baptism and celebrate the Eucharist of the Lord. But the word does not first reach its effect only when it becomes specific in the actual word of preaching and in the sacrament which relate to the individual. For wherever grace happens in the world, outside the individual events of word and sacrament, it has already achieved its categorical, salvation-historical actuality in the basic sacrament of the Church.

Following from this fundamental understanding, a new "experience" of the Church now becomes comprehensible, namely, the experience that the Church is the basic sacrament of the world's salvation precisely where the world is not the Church. Today and tomorrow's Christian will not experience *ecclesial* Christianity first and foremost as just one of the many world views which one can find in the world marketplace; nor will he consider it to be a sum of theories which, on the level of categorical statements, is against or opposes all other theoretical reflexions on the existence of man. Rather, the Catholic Christian must experience the Church as the vanguard, as the sacramental sign, as the historical reality of a saving grace which goes beyond what is sociologically tangible, which goes beyond being a "visible Church"; he must also experience the Church as the historical, tangible reality of an anonymous Christianness which, "outside" the Church, has not yet fully found itself, but which, "inside" the Church, does find itself—and this is so not because it absolutely does not exist outside the Church, but because there it has not in an objective way reached its full-flowering, and therefore does not yet fully comprehend itself in the explicitness and reflexive objectivity of a formal creed, in the objectivity of a sacramental making-present, and in the objectivity of social organization, such as all this occurs in the Church.

What we mean to say, if we may simplify the matter (and we will not here consider the question of the non-Catholic Christian), is that the Christian will not regard the non-Christian as standing outside the pale of salvation simply because he is not a Christian. If it is true that Christianity is salvation, and that God does not, in view of salvation, capriciously allow good intentions to count for the act itself (which would contravene the doctrine of the mediational and not only the mandatory necessity of Church and grace), —if all this is true, then the Christian will see the non-Christian as an anonymous Christian who does not really know what he actually is through grace in the depths of his conscience; that is, that the anonymous Christian is, in perhaps a very implicit but nevertheless in a very real way, what the Christian also is, though for his part the Christian is aware of what he is in the objective reflexiveness of his conscience.

There can be no doubt, of course, that this objective reflexiveness, this explicit, creed-like, formulated faith is a part of the whole Christianity, that it is a grace which ensures and facilitates that what is thus confessed is truly made present in the depths of being and conscience. There can be no doubt that the Catholic rightly perceives and praises his express belonging to the Church as an undeserved grace, as a blessing, as a promise of salvation (though at the same time knowing with profound alarm that the greater grace is at the same time the greater danger). He will know that more is asked of him to whom more is given, that more is asked of him who does not really know whether he has fully done that which was asked *of him*. He will remember in terror the words of the Lord: that many will come out of the east and out of the west, but that the children of the kingdom will be cast forth into darkness (Mt. 8, 11f.).

The *Constitution on the Church,* too, with a word of St. Augustine (Art. 14), distinguishes between belonging to the Church *"corde"* (with the heart) and belonging *"corpore"* (in body). The Catholic Christian knows that he belongs *corpore* to the Church; but whether he lives *corde* in the Church through faithful love, this he does not know, surely; this he can—must—only hope. But because the Christian also hopes for the salvation of others; because he knows enough, theologically, to see that he may *hope* for their salvation (even though he knows that it is not beyond doubt); because today he can more readily see, theologically, how it is possible to be a Christian (we use the word here to mean one living in the grace of God and his Christ) even without knowing the name of Christ, or even while thinking that Christ must be rejected, —*because* of all this, he can see himself and all who are called Christian members of the Church only as the vanguard of those who wander along the roads of history towards the salvation of God and into his eternity. He will know that the light upon the mountains is the dawn of day in the valley below.

In view of the Christian teaching that there is no absolute evil principle, that evil is nothingness, that the only God is good and desires the good of the world, that the real is also good, and therefore that true realism must think well of reality, —in view of this, the Christian will know that it would be blasphemy to imagine that ultimately the bad is more easily done than the good. He will deny that a "sober" and "realistic" view of reality sees it ultimately as evil and not as good. He will not admit that good, so to speak, is "short of breath," and evil "long-winded." He will know that it is not the humility but the pride of the creature which thinks that at least in evil it can emancipate itself from God.

He will know that this is a stupid lie. He will know that it is the accomplishment of existence which is asked of him: that in the darkness he will be asked to believe in the light, in anguish to believe in bliss, in his relativity to believe in the absoluteness of God. He will know that revelation in our history has unmasked our sins only that we might believe in the forgiveness of God (for our guilt alone we could already have come to know from our pain, our death, and our destitution).

When St. Paul sees the unbelief of the Jews as temporary (Rom. 9–11), this does not mean (at least for a theology which no longer wishes to think merely "collectively" and yet wishes to agree with St. Paul) that only the Jews of some later date were to become believers, while the Jews of St. Paul's time were simply to remain *un*believers. Only an un-Christian collectivist could view the situation in so simplified a way (and this regardless of whether St. Paul himself develops to the end or not the thought which forms the core of his contemplation: the triumph of God's grace over unbelief). What this Pauline text means is that the faith of the people of Israel which is to become actual at some later historical date (and even then, not in some tangible way, not as some kind of guarantee of individual salvation) will be a sign that God has already had mercy on this people in some incomprehensible way (and again, this will have nothing to do with individual mercy). For why else would Israel as a whole be spoken of in light of her faith of some later time, and not in light of her unbelief of an earlier time? How else could one truly say, "Israel is founded on the grace of God," and not: "This people has denied itself to God"?

This is why the Christian looks forth tranquilly and without fear into the world. He need not restlessly check statistics to see whether the Church is really the largest single organized world view, whether she grows at a rate proportionate to (or greater than) the increase in the world's population. Of course, the Christian will look forth into the world with missionary zeal, just as the *Constitution on the Church* and the *Decree on the Church's Missionary Activity* carefully see to it that their astonishing optimism about salvation does not obscure the missionary task of the Church or weaken the missionary zeal of Christians. (Even so, however, there does remain the question, which we will not take up here, whether there is any clear "synthesis" of ideas regarding that optimism about salvation on the one hand, and the missionary obligation on the other.)

In any case, the Christian will bear witness to the name of Christ. He will want to share his grace with others, for he possesses a grace which the others lack, which they *yet* lack, namely, the grace to belong to the Church "*corpore*" and not only "*corde*," so that then they too may contribute to that sacramental basic sign which is the Church, who calls the whole world in freedom and reality to make room in human existence for that divine life which has always been at work in the base of the human person. For this divine life, the self-revelation of the Word, impels history towards its blessed perfection, and it desires to appear incarnated in history in full measure.

The Christian knows, therefore, that if in his missionary activity he is zealous patiently, then his zeal has the greatest chance for success. He knows that he should imitate the forebearance of God (which, according to St. Paul, is of a positively salvific rather than of a judicial nature). He knows that God wanted the world to be just the way it is, or else the world would not be; and that even the "merely" *permitted* is permitted only as a moment of a divine state. And he knows that this divine state may be hoped for, must be hoped for, not only as the revelation of the justice of God, but also as the revelation of his immense grace to mankind.

The Christian knows that God does not begin his work of grace only when man begins it in God's name. Therefore, he will confront in courage and hope and as brother even that man who does not want to be his brother. He will see that man as someone who does not fully realize what he is, what presumably has already begun to take place in the depths of his existence—and we mean that it is the Christian's duty to *presume* in hope that God's grace is at work in his brother's existence, for to think otherwise would show a lack of love on his part. (For may I as a Christian assume that another man is outside the grace of God?)

The Christian sees anonymous Christianity at work in a thousand ways in his brother. If he knows that man is ever growing, ever perfecting himself in his existence, more than he can ever himself explain, then the Christian can never consider it indiscreet to postulate in the non-Christian an anonymous Christianity as pre-given in grace or even as subconsciously perfected (even if this is contrary to the non-Christian's own interpretation of his existence). If the Christian interprets *himself* (correctly understood) as *"simul justus et peccator"* or therefore also as *"simul fidelis et infidelis,"* although he wants to be *"fidelis"* and only that, then it is also no impudence to understand the non-Christian as perhaps *"simul fidelis"* even though he wants to be only *"infidelis."*

If the Christian sees the non-Christian as kind, loving, true to his conscience, he will no longer say that these are "natural virtues." For natural virtues ultimately exist only *in abstracto.* He will no longer say, as St. Augustine did, that they are the "glittering vices of the heathen." Much rather will he say: here the grace of Christ is at work in a man who never expressly asked for it, but who already desired it in the unspeaking, nameless longing of his heart. Here is a man in whom the unspeaking sighing of the Spirit has invoked and petitioned for that silent but all-pervading mystery of existence which we Christians know as the Father of our Lord Jesus Christ.

If the Christian sees the heathen die willingly, if he sees how the heathen, as if there were no other way (and oh, there are other ways, for one can use the last powers of one's entire existence for absolute protest and absolute cynical doubt), willingly allows himself in death to plunge into the bottomless abyss and confess that this abyss is the abyss of significant mystery and not the damning void, —if he sees this, the Christian sees in the dying man the figure of the one crucified at the right hand of Jesus on the salvation-bringing cross of existence; he will see that this dying man is bringing to full perfection and reality his entire existence as he wordlessly says, "Jesus, remember me when you come in your kingly power."

And why should it not be so? The pure transcendence of man, now no longer used as a means of asserting one's earthly existence but rather accepted and endured, can certainly be exalted by grace so that, liberated from its contortion into the future, it becomes the dynamic factor which impels man towards the God of eternal life.

This sovereign and liberating orientation of the spiritual transcendence of man by grace (for according to good Thomistic teaching it alters the horizon, the formal object of spiritual perfection, even if it does not set forward a concrete new object) is in actuality a "revelation" (and not a "natural" revelation), a revelation that is grace-giving, free, personal (and to that extent verbalized), from God—and, therefore, when accepted: faith.

Why then should the obedient and loving engagement of a person, in the inaccessible infinity of his transcendence (which one does not engage in to the degree that he comprehends it, but in accordance with one's being apprehended by the infinity beyond one's control), not be, within the present order of God's supernatural will for the salvation of man, more than merely such a mere spiritual-natural transcendence? Why should it not, in fact, through the action of God, be for us the dynamic which transports us into the life of God? And why should it not suffice that man accept this dynamic in the very fact of willingly allowing the incomprehensible to have disposition over him in his uncomprehendingness? (Must it be particularly emphasized that all the demands of the natural and supernatural ethic are to be thought of as implicitly contained therein? Of course, contained in such a manner that, as the experience of the heathen shows—but also of the Christian—the genuine orientation towards God can be existentially "subjectively" accomplished even where the most consequential errors are to be found with reference to material in individual norms of morality.)

Thus when the Christian now preaches Christianity to the non-Christian, he will no longer proceed so much from the idea of transforming the other into something which he plainly has not been heretofore, but rather he will attempt to bring him to himself. Not, of course, in the Modernistic sense that Christianity is simply the explanation of a natural religious need, but because God, on account of his general will that all men be saved, already long ago offered man in this grace the most actual, the most ultimate reality of Christianity, and because it is absolutely possible and probable that this man has already freely accepted this reality even without knowing it in a reflexive way.

It is under these presuppositions, then, that the Christian of today and tomorrow will see and experience the Church.

He will experience it not as something rare, asserting itself only with great ardor; not as one of the many "sects" or world views into which man is divided; not as one of the numberless divisions of pluralistic society. Rather, the Church will appear to the Christian far more as the actualization, as the concretization of something which already demands interior commitment, as the historical constitutionalization of the universal and of the actually self-evident; as the pure representation of the being of man as planned by God (of the "historical" being of man, of which the supernatural vocation is a part); in short, as the *basic sacrament* of a grace which, for the very reason that it is offered to all, urges to its sacramental historicity even where the individual sacrament (baptism) is not yet given.

Consequently, grace is never simply *identical* with its own effective sign; but rather, through the individual sign which it makes present and by which it is made present (both must be stated), it gives assurance that it is *everywhere* powerful. We may safely say, therefore, that the grace of God gives assurance through the individual sacramental sign; that it is everywhere powerful, even where this individual sacramental sign as such does not yet reach those very men in whom we may hope that the grace of God is very powerfully at work. For these individual signs taken collectively constitute the Church (in unity, that is, with other Church-forming factors), because the Church is the communion of those who are baptized and who celebrate the Eucharist.

Moreover, the Church as the *sacramentum* of the world's salvation, is the promise of grace to the world. If the history of mankind is a unified one, a history in which everything is somehow related, from Abel down to the last man, a history in which each man is significant for all other men for all time (and not only, in other words, for our this-worldly time and space), —then the Church is truly the leavened dough not only where she has grasped a handful of the remaining flour visible for all our eyes to see (and thereby making each handful again a part of the fermentation process), —she is not only this, but exists always for all people, for every time and most especially where the flour is still not a part of the leavened dough (that is, insofar as that flour does not appear to be part of the leavened dough).

Thus the Church in her new image will appear to the Christian as the promise to the non-Christian world. And she will appear as promise not only insofar as the world has already become the Church. For this promise is not the promise merely of a growing Church, a Church becoming of this world; but rather, it is the genuine hope of the world for a possibility of salvation through the Church.

4. The Community of Love

It is in the context of the Church considered as the community of love that the most profound basis of the collegial-synodal principle in the Church first becomes clear. And the basis is this: the love of those who are unified and assimilated in Christ in community, even though there is hierarchical differentiation in the community—for the basis of this hierarchy is itself love. The union of love in the Spirit, the God-given fraternity, has of course always been in itself the center and the goal of the Gospel message and of service in the Church. For she has always known and taught that love of God and love of neighbor are one and the same commandment, are the one grace which justifies. And yet, this incomprehensible self-evident fact which constitutes the mystery of our existence will determine in a totally new way the image of the Church and of ecclesial piety.

The usual clichés about today's mass society may be considered false, onesided, or premature, but they do point to a danger: that precisely on account of the ever greater social entanglement, on account of the ever growing immensity of existence, on account of the increasing specialization of the function of the individual in society, —precisely on account of all this, the individual himself can find no concrete thou, no space for intimacy that does not mean abandonment or aloneness, but finds himself instead to be an anonymous, shifting, insignificant part of a gigantic social apparatus.

Of course, outside of the ecclesial sphere and independently of the Church there are other groups of men which attempt to mediate a protective nearness of man to man; and certainly the family will emphatically achieve this, its oldest and newest significance, by being always the locus of personal and unique love. But for that same reason, the local

Church, as the community of love, gathered round the altar of Christ, can achieve a totally new significance precisely when the local Church of the future no longer appears to be primarily some administrative outpost of some immeasurable megalo-organization purportedly set up for the salvation of the soul of the individual.

The Church as local community will be the community of those free in faith, of personal decision, for whom baptism is the expression and manifestation of grace, or at least of the acceptance into a family and a community of the faithful, in which the faith of those coming of age can truly mature in a personal way. In such a community that brotherliness will thrive which is founded in Christ. This community will certainly not be able to consider itself as some kind of "other-worldly" sect not really needing to concern itself with the cares of the world, some kind of hideaway on the fringe of the world. If such a community experiences itself as the sacrament of the world's salvation, it will *not*, moreover, be able fully to understand its task as witness, its function as salt and leavened dough in the world, its mission into every sphere of human life. But that does not mean that it cannot truly discover itself as the community of fraternity in Christ.

By comparison with the physical (and yes, even the ideological) power of the future world states, or the future world state, even the universal Church will have less historical power than it now proportionately has—if by power we understand that possibility of determining a man in a way that can preclude truth and love. The pastors and officials of the Church, therefore, with all the natural recognition of their spiritual plenipotence, will no longer be seen as bearers of social power. For the plenipotence of office comes from the mission of Christ; the true meaning of office rests solely upon love. The office will unite, therefore, all those who share the experience of the love of Christ in community; and it will be in this way that a genuinely familial exchange between laymen and clergy will come about, as the *Constitution* describes it (Art. 37). This essential characteristic of the new image of the Church will be all that remains of the institutional. In the local community of the future the unity of love of God and neighbor will be experienced entirely anew. God will not be demythologized down to the level of man, but in the Christianity of the man-becoming of God, God will be found in man; and man will be discovered as the mystery existing into the mystery of God, finding God's true essence only in that which man himself is not, and thus come to know in love what is meant by "God."

To be sure, we have now only a vague and indistinct idea of what such a community of love of God and neighbor will be like, how it will concretely be, how an altar community can be molded, how there can be a community which is neither a neighborhood group that weekly gets together in church, nor a lonely-hearts club for the socially frustrated, nor yet a very sophisticated warehouse where the individual person can procure the moral fortification requisite for his individual salvation.

The community of the new Church must be a community of love, and love is very concrete. But it is better for us to admit at this point that we honestly don't know what such a community of love will be like. For only when we do not yet feel that we possess, are we capable of acquiring.

5. Other Features of the New Image of the Church

All that we have described above does not, of course, exhaust the number of features of the new image of the Church as it can be discovered, at least in rudimentary form, in the ecclesiology of the Second Vatican Council. This is true particularly since what is most primary always remains what is the most new. The oldest and newest thing in the Church is what she herself says and mediates; but the Church does not say herself; rather, she is the word which speaks of the Other, and she renders this Other present and effective for us.

Ecclesiology is, therefore, to the other treatises of dogmatics what grammar, poetics, and semantics are to poetry. The Church understands herself best when she perfects herself: and this means, when she speaks of God and his grace, of Jesus Christ and his cross and resurrection, of everlasting life, when she allows herself to be seized by the grace of this word which she speaks.

Or we might put it this way: the Church comprehends what she is as the institution of salvation only when she understands and perfects herself as the *fruit* of salvation.

There is no doubt, moreover, that the *Constitution on the Church* has understood this fact, for it speaks at length (and why not?) about the Church as institution, about her offices and powers, about her hierarchical structure, about her didactic and pastoral offices, about the many apostolates in the Church's mission—that is, in sum, about the Church as institution and mediation of salvation. But behind all this is the much more basic understanding that the Church is the people of God gathered by the grace of God, an outgrowth of God's grace, the fruit of salvation.

If the Church intends to see herself as the body of Christ, as the people of God, as the "wandering people of God," herself still a pilgrim in history on her way to the far-off goal; if she comprehends herself as a reality which has the appearance of this world (Art. 48) and still desires to lift herself to that level where the kingdom of God is "all in all" and no longer the Church; if all the bearers of hierarchical power are seen to be who they are *because the Church is,* and not as those who "form" the Church, —if all of this is true, then certainly shall the Church overcome that onesided view of her as an authoritative institution of salvation, then certainly will she appear to be not some kind of regulatory body but rather as something *which we all are*—for God's grace has been given to us, and unites us.

Let us therefore name but a few more features of the new image of the Church. For more than in the magisterial ecclesiology of earlier days, the Church now appears as the sinful Church of sinners, constantly in need of converting herself to the Lord (even though in the *Constitution* this theme did not receive its full share of consideration). What new features, then, does the *Constitution* describe?

First of all, the Church appears as the communion of faith, of hope, and of love (Arts. 8, 64, 65), as the Church of the Trinity. Moreover, she is not just the Church of hierarchical power and of the sacraments, but also the Church of the charismatics (Art. 12), the Church of martyrs (Art. 42). The Church sees herself as the Church of the poor and the oppressed (Arts. 8, 41). In the *Constitution* she overcomes much more distinctly than ever before the misconception that the distinction between clergy and laity or between the religious and lay life automatically implies a difference in a man's nearness to God, in his love of God and neighbor.

Moreover, the Church knows herself to be the Church of the eschatological era of salvation history, an era in which for faith the dramatic dialogue between God and man is already irrevocably decided by God in favor of the salvation of man (Art. 48). But she knows also that she is not yet a full part of this era, that she is still a part of that creation which anxiously awaits the revelation of the glory of the children of God.

The Church, then, is not merely some immobile institution of salvation which mediates to the individual receivers of salvation the future kingdom of God and their eternal life. Rather, she is the pilgrim, herself wandering through history towards that eternity in which she will no longer be as such the authoritative and sacramental institution of salvation (Art. 48).

We have been able to list only a few of the new features of the new image of the Church. It should not be surmised, however, that other, more familiar features of the past are no longer valid or meaningful in this new image. Moreover, it goes without saying that the existential realization of these new features still demands a long period of trial by error until they become truly and vividly apparent to the ecclesial piety of the individual, and in the practice of the Church.

But a beginning in this ecclesial piety has been made. All now depends on the true transformation of the letter of the conciliar ecclesiology into spirit and life.

THEOLOGY
A NEW CHALLENGE

CHAPTER THREE

THE Second Vatican Council is without doubt an immense challenge for Catholic theology, for it has presented it with new tasks, a profounder dynamic, and greater freedom of movement. But the Council is a challenge above all because of the theological significance of its teachings.

Before the Council was convened, many Roman Catholic theologians thought—and many more feared—that the Council would merely reiterate the official papal teaching and the traditional theology of neo-Scholastic origin which has been explicitly professed throughout the preceding century. In this way, the post-conciliar theology might merely have passed on in further editions of Denzinger the extant body of doctrine, embellished now with polite references to the new Council texts. Of course, this is not what actually happened, though to be sure the Council was cautious and discreet in its doctrinal statements, and even avoided defining any new dogma. On the other hand, however, it had much to say which was not merely a part of the matter-of-course repertory of Scholastic theology.

With good reason, the Council wished to assert only truths which have always been present in some way (if in varying degrees of reflexiveness) in the consciousness of the Church. And from this standpoint, nothing that the Council teaches can be said to be absolutely "new." But this still does not mean it had to limit itself to the repertory of the Scholastic theology of the past century (even if, in fact, the present consciousness of faith of the Church and the religious practice of her people are nourished by an explicitly formulated, historically conditioned Scholastic theology). For example, in few dogmatic texts or diocesan catechisms of the recent past can there be found a statement to the effect that the sacrament of penance is also a reconciliation with the Church herself—although this is most clearly a part of ancient tradition. (Where such a doctrine is at all mentioned, moreover, it is only by way of objecting to it.) The logical consequence is that truth plays no practical part in the life of the Christian of today. It was highly significant, therefore, that the Council should have suddenly broken through the pattern of recent dogmatic tracts and catechisms, and call back to life realities and truths which simply were not alive in the Church and the theology of yesterday.

What is decisive here is not so much the fact that many controversial questions were taken up and, to a certain extent, answered at the Council—thereby setting for theology the task of thinking through these answers, justifying them, and clarifying any remaining obscurities. Far more important is the fact that much of what was taught by the Council was not actually controversial in Scholastic theology, but was at the same time not clearly formulated, —so that it could find no room in the catechisms shaped by that theology, nor any room in the day-to-day consciousness of the believing Christian.

Thus the Council has provided theology with themes and tasks of no little significance, and signaled its responsibility for expanding and in no small measure of restructuring its own over-all make-up and methods.

Beyond this, however, the Council is significant for theology in another, twofold respect. For the Council deliberately left a number of theological questions open, or else opened them, or expressly recognized them as subject to further investigation. And these were not only questions which have no real significance for the concrete life of the Church or the Christian existence of men, theological subtleties concerning the professional theologian and his introverted preoccupations. The question regarding the collegiality of the bishops, for example, was so sharply controversial not because it could be seriously and factually doubted, but because of the sudden theological discovery of the concrete, practical consequences of this doctrine, which even the "infallibilists" of Vatican I never contested theoretically, but on the contrary categorically taught.

Alongside this expansion of the theological role, this intensification of theological discourse, the Council exhibited in its very mentality a new spirit of freedom, a desire first to examine and only then to decide (according to the formula of Paul VI), an awareness of problems, a certain respect for professional theologians (without, however, timidly leaving the last word to their "professional" bias). Thus the theological routine which was the order of the day in the past century, operating in the conviction that everything of real importance in theology had already been settled, has now been shaken off—that is, provided that theology really takes advantage of the opportunity presented it by the Council. It would surely seem, for example (if we may be allowed to digress for a moment in support of our contention), that the sheer amount of theological study on the Mariological question in the last decades (no matter how praiseworthy) was *also* (and not *only*) indicative of the implicit understanding that progress (in retrospective dogmatic history) was still possible solely in the outskirts of theology. A dogmatic historian of the stature of a Landgraf actually stated such an opinion in the course of private conversation. Moreover, one might even be of the opinion that, as for example in the encyclical *Humani generis,* the legitimate defense of theological concepts whose historical evolution is accepted, but which once formulated are considered in every respect immutable, was also inspired by a mentality which saw theology as evolved but at the same time (except for peripheral matters) simply completed. The Council has shown that such a mentality is no longer legitimate today (at least it did so in its ecclesiology and in the *Dogmatic Constitution on Divine Revelation*). Surely the Council has offered to theology an intensified awareness of problems and a greater leeway for free theological investigation.

Theology has reaped yet another advantage from the

Council, beyond the formality of a general theological orientation. For the Council has initiated the dialogue with the world. It has not, of course—and to be sure could not have by itself—accomplished this dialogue. But the Council has begun to see, to recognize the spirit of today's world, that is, of a world which is pluralistic, scientific, technological, of tremendous scope and diversity in knowledge and direction, a world of shattered Christianity, of many religions, a world of a tremendously projected future. And it is not a world in which one simply lives, either in delight or dismay, in order to devote oneself only to the old inherited tasks and goals. Rather, it is a world with which one must enter into an open dialogue (a dialogue, that is, whose outcome is not predetermined); it is a world which the Church must help to shape, but also a world which in turn will help to shape the Church, and this in a way which will not merely be tolerated by but expressly desired by the Church.

This developing situation, now recognized and accepted by the Church, does not simply imply (though it does that also) a new, additional, though constricted task for theology, that is to say, involvement in the question as posed and thematically outlined in the *Pastoral Constitution on the Church in the Modern World*. Rather, this dialogue with the world, in which the Church must take an explicit stand, implies a task for theology seen in its entire range, even in those dimensions which at first might seem to be somewhat esoteric. For if theology has been given a new task, this means that each of the parts of theology must come to understand this concept, divine its significance, and work together for its realization.

On the basis of these prefatory remarks, therefore, we shall now attempt to say something about the task of post-conciliar theology. We are aware, of course, of the fragmentary and subjective nature of our remarks. We also know that making demands is a painful business, that it is easier to give counsel than to abide by it, that only he gives true prescription who also clearly indicates its application.

With regard to historical theology in general, we must first urgently and seriously stress the fact that it must be further extended and developed. If Catholic theology has advanced in the past century—and we here disregard biblical science, which we will consider separately later on—then it was especially, if not almost exclusively, in the areas of historical theology, of dogmatic and theological history, of patristic literary history, of textual exegesis, of juridical history, and the like. There is no doubt, moreover, that sufficient further tasks remain to historical theology. No Scholastic science, especially today, can dispense with the pursuit of its own history. Theology owes this concern to its own sublime dignity. Where talent in this direction is available (and there are some who are suitable more or less only for that), it ought to be fostered. Nor would it be amiss were the Church authorities to be in the future somewhat more liberal, financially, in this respect (for example, for the purpose of publishing specialized books, or the printing of special historical investigations). Furthermore, it would not necessarily be detrimental to the dignity of this historical theology and its disinterested research of the truth, if in the future it were to become more conscious of its function and responsibility in the light of what is called "systematic" theology—and this includes "practical," or pastoral theology, for so-called systematic theology is true to its purpose only when it serves the truly vital kerygma of the Gospel and the Christian existence of today, and when it is motivated by an awareness of the deficiencies in the pastoral ministry.

If we consider the elite of historical theology in the last century—Ehrle, Denifle, Bardenhewer, Grabmann, Pelster, Landgraf, among others—we must soberly admit, if we are to be truthful, that their great and scholarly work on the proclamation of the salvific message of Christ is, for any practical purpose, of no use today. Their historical theology was restrospective theology, and this singular orientation to the past can be of no present value. We need only to think of a Congar, a Chenu, or a de Lubac for examples of historical theology which is of immense practical importance.

Historical theology, in other words, as a whole can no longer be so antique, so retrospective, in its inclination. On the contrary, it must become far more prospective, it must regress only to reach forward to a new future for theology and kerygma. Historical theology may not simply ask what happened: it must question the past in order to discover what will be, what must be proclaimed tomorrow.

Historical theology must come to boast, therefore, of its theologians who sympathize and identify with the mission, the unrest, the burden, and the hazard of the theology of today in view of the kerygma of tomorrow. In the theological exercise which time and the Council have prescribed for him for tomorrow, the historical theologian must certainly ask most earnestly what happened, but he can no longer affect a kind of "art-for-art's-sake" attitude, he must learn to diminish his previous extravagant historical curiosity. Rather, he must come to inquire of the past what questions on life and death the future poses for theology, even if, as a result, some *quodlibits* of second- and third-rate medieval theologians remain unedited and unreviewed.

If it is to be fruitful for systematic theology, such historical investigation must especially learn to listen to the past with an unprejudiced ear—even if, at first, the past may not seem to have much to say which is interesting or of "existential" significance. Without this patient listening, historical theology would ultimately hear only what it already knows. But it must learn to endure listening to the seemingly dull and long-familiar tradition in order to discover something new. This, quite emphatically, does not mean that the theologian, as theologian (that is, as being more than a religious historian), —who must always listen to the past with a contemporary understanding—, may confine himself to understanding only those aspects of faith which have become actual and which are now being practiced. He must not come to think that his horizon is categorically static, stationed somewhere in the "present," reaching neither fully into the past nor fully into the future. Rather, his understanding must concern itself with those aspects of Christian life and faith which are in the process of *becoming,* which are announced in the promise of the past, and which are required to become real by the obtruding need of the future.

Today's theologian should not attempt to demonstrate his scholarship—even in the field of history—by writing books which no one except his closest colleagues and successors would read and on topics which are of no abiding significance to anyone but himself. His must not simply demonstrate, so very thoroughly, that someone from the past already knew beforehand something which was only defined at some later (even much later) date. For it is all really unnecessary. A more important task for the historical theologian is to pry loose from the past new perspectives on the problems which face theology today, to help elicit an increased awareness of how these problems must be resolved for tomorrow, and he must do this even if the shell of the past withstands nearly all the might of his lever. For if the historical theologian is truly motivated by an interest in the present situation of a problem, and its future, and not only in its past, it is likely that he will force out of the past (though rarely in full measure, and usually only to a degree) an affirmation on a point of doctrine which even today is without the definitive authorization of the Church; and it is possible that this very affirmation may alter the significance of this doctrinal point in the systematic Scholastic theology of today.

But even if such occasional breakthroughs are not

achieved, such historical investigation can well serve today's systematic theology, for, to recapitulate, it can help to intensify the awareness that problems do exist; it can help to illustrate the indirection, the aporia of much of today's valid dogma, and indicate that a new integration and synthesis can be made within a framework that has been broadened by the new possibilities for interpretation provided by the contemporary situation; and it can help clarify the difference between dogma and its ever-present cousin, theological opinion.

All of this is true for historical theology especially in the fields of moral theology and Canon Law. In these areas historical theology can still be very useful, and in fact necessary (for this is proved by the present development of both of these disciplines), by calling into question various theses in systematic theology which have, even if in good historical conscience, been too much oversimplified, too complacently rendered. The same might perhaps also be said of ecclesiastical history, even though the practical application of this discipline is difficult to discern or put into effect. (One could very easily have had the impression, however, while attending the Council debates, that many of the Fathers had very little knowledge of the history of the Church, of the history of its organization and habits, and even of much of its doctrine—or at least that they had learned very little from it.)

Biblical science has also been provided with many great new tasks by the Council. This is so not because these tasks did not exist before now, but because the possibilities for finding new solutions have been improved, and above all been made more secure. The *Dogmatic Constitution on Divine Revelation* was certainly cautious and conservative in the development of its teaching, but it is nonetheless a constitution of great significance for biblical science: for in this area the newest is not necessarily the most valid and lasting. And there will surely be, in the coming decades, an immense need for biblical theologians to have the courage to uphold the need for freedom in the practice of the Christian faith; and this courage will not take form in the defense of positions which are merely traditional, but rather of the kind which will resist that historical skepticism which, almost inevitably, runs parallel with any modern historical science. In the case of biblical science, its skeptics will imagine that, without any genuine religious experience, they can adequately deduce from its parts and its historical assumptions the living whole of the truth of faith; or they will fancy that, where this is not possible, a dogma or its meaning as maintained by the Church is no longer binding.

In any case, the *Dogmatic Constitution on Divine Revelation* sanctioned the development of biblical science that had been given its first impetus under the pontificate of Pius XII (in *Divino afflante Spiritu* and in certain explanations of the Biblical Commission). It is now generally accepted, for example, that in exegesis and in the biblical theology of the Old and New Testaments, Catholic exegetes may use to advantage many of the methods developed by evangelical biblical science, notably regarding the history of form, for there is nothing in these methods as such which is dogmatically unacceptable. And even if one adheres to the "historicity" of the four Gospels, this rather global qualification of the Gospels must be modified along the lines of the *Dogmatic Constitution on Divine Revelation,* which has recognized a *vario modo historicum* regarding the Gospels, and which also took into account the fact that post-Easter theology helped shape the reports concerning the pre-Easter Jesus.

The crucial task of biblical theological investigation must be to show that there is a profound difference, and yet at the same time a real relationship (which will be sufficient for the demands of Catholic dogma), between the historical Jesus and the Christ of faith of St. John and St. Paul. For the man of today, with all his historical staidness and his eye for difference and development, can see with his eye of faith more in the history of Jesus than the life and fate of some religious fanatic. And this is no merely apologetical task, a defense such as that undertaken by de Grandmaison some forty years ago. The clarification of the contrast between what the Church teaches about Jesus and what Jesus said about himself—and this contrast abolishes neither the substantial oneness nor the uniqueness of the two—can truly have a positive effect on dogmatic Christology. For it compels Christology to a radical seriousness when it considers the true humanity of Jesus, his human subjectivity and historical circumstances; and to a more precise realization that the hypostatic union does not lesson the true humanity of Jesus, but radicalizes it, and establishes its supreme perfection and independence from God.

For biblical theology to have such a positive effect on dogmatic Christology, it is indeed requisite that there be closer collaboration between exegesis and dogmatics than has been the case in past years. Moreover, in participating in this collaborative venture, the dogmatic theologian should realize that it is not actually possible for the biblical exegete, if he is sincere and painstaking in his work, to come up with a-historical, fabricated findings; and he must show, more adequately than heretofore, that for a correct understanding of the Christological dogma (one which has been now "demythologized"), the genuine findings of the exegete are certainly sufficient as the point of departure, as the foundation for dogmatics.

This collaboration is of great practical significance for today's kerygma in that only by this means can Christology develop in a way which is acceptable to the scientific understanding and Christian faith of men of today.

Moreover, the *Decree on Priestly Formation* has assigned to Catholic biblical science a far greater and more basic task than that of preparing the *dicta probantia* for those various theses (and their selection and system) which are presupposed in exegesis. Biblical theology is now enjoined to determine, *by its own examination of the Scriptures,* what ought to be thematic for systematic theology; that is, it ought not simply to situate the biblical-theological material in some Scholastically predetermined framework (as is the case, for instance, even in the "biblical theology" of a von Cüppens). There can be no doubt that such a *posteriori* synthetic method, in contrast to the previous analytical-Scholastic method (in which a thesis is postulated, analyzed, and then tested against the sources), will considerably enrich and alter the thematics of dogmatic theology. Themes such as the theology of history, the theology of the word, and the hermeneutics of theological predicates in general will then be easily placed within the framework of systematic theology. To take a small but important example: presumably there is to the present day not one Catholic Scholastic ecclesiology which develops a theology of the local Church as the manifestation and concrete actuality of the Church as a whole (although the *Dogmatic Constitution on the Church* exhorts to just such a theology). But such a teaching would be a matter of course in a dogmatic ecclesiology which derived its thematics from biblical theology. It is, therefore, an important business for biblical science to heed the Council's official command to be in a certain sense the mistress and not just the handmaid of dogmatic theology.

There is much more that we could say regarding systematic theology, specifically as it concerns dogmatics and moral theology, but we must now turn our attention to a matter which we have just only briefly touched on, namely, ecclesiology.

It is evident, as we review the conciliar texts, that the Council with good reason issued many a mandate by virtue of its explicit teachings. One such "mandate" was that theology must now be concerned above all with *conciliar* ecclesiology. Of course, the Council formulated its teachings on the Church in accordance with traditional teachings, but this does not mean that it did not bring to the forefront of theological awareness many ecclesiological themes which are worthy and in need of further examination, and which, in fact, entail a number of practical consequences. We will name only a few such themes, though we list them without any systematization or logical ordering: the more precise relationship of the primacy of the pope to the episcopal college; the nature of the ordinary teaching office; the relationship between Scripture and tradition; the pneumatic-sacramental substantiation of justice in the Church; the role of charisma in the Church; the theology of the diaconate; the eschatological character of the Church; the possibility of the salvation of non-Christians; the ecclesiological aspect of penance (and of the sacraments in general); the nature of revelation and of salvation history; the synodal principle in the Church in general; the ecclesiological place of the evangelical counsels and of religious orders in the Church; the significance and relevance of the concept of a hierarchy of the truths of revelation; the theology of the missions; the possibility of a *communicatio in sacris* between separated Christians; the theology of the function of non-Christian religions in collective and individual salvation history; the obligation of the pope (even if it cannot be juridically standardized further) to make use of the collegial organs of the Church; the theology of the local community and the community of the altar as Church; the possibility of a historical development of the *jus divinum* in apostolic times; the theology of the word and theological hermeneutics; the Church as *sacramentum salus mundi;* the theology of sin in the Church; the theology of the historicity of the ecclesial recognition of truth and the fallibility of this recognition; —these and many more themes, in the widest sense of the word "ecclesiological," have been newly presented to theology by the Council.

Systematic theology, besides its task of having to comment directly on the theological texts of the Council, will also have to engage in a thorough study of ecclesiological themes such as we have listed above. And in the attempt at solution of ecclesiological problems, systematic theology will have to go far beyond what was explicit and commonplace in the traditional theology before the Council. We repeat, it can no longer be validly maintained that today's systematic theology can break new ground (apart from historical retrospection) only in such fringe areas as Mariology, because, as it is argued, everything is more or less crystal-clear, and cannot be said any better than the way it is already being said.

Perhaps we are mistaken, but we see the description of future moral theology as it is expressed in the *Decree on Priestly Formation* as a severe but just criticism of the current moral theology taught in the seminaries. In the *Decree on Priestly Formation,* the mission and method of moral theology are conceived in a manner quite unlike their seminarial counterparts. For Article 16 of this decree prescribes

92

moral-theological biblical theology; it prescribes a positive orientation of all moral theology towards love; it prescribes the suppression of an insular concern for the salvation of the individual; it prescribes a morality of service to the world; and all these, heretofore, have not been part of the moral theology of the seminary textbooks.

It would be obvious and tempting—but ultimately a fatal mistake—to imagine that the chief task of systematic theology in the coming decades will be the annotation of the conciliar texts, and the historical justification and the systematic organization of the themes explicitly dealt with by the Council. Such a development of theology in the coming years would be incommensurate with the Council's spirit and intention. The Council had no wish to invite theology to become the way and means of an introversion of the Church upon herself. The Council wished to confront the Church of today both inexorably and courageously. That was the real purpose of the Second Vatican Council. But this situation of a Church wanting to find the man of today, and having no desire of being a historical relic of a bygone sociological day, gives rise to far more radical questions than simply those which relate to a more subtle ecclesiology, or to any of the other themes explicitly treated by the Council.

The newest questions are at the same time the oldest and the most radically fundamental ones for Christianity. In the first place, the question of the existence of God, whose answer implies a theology of atheism and of unbelief in general, a question which—in the unity of a transcendental inquiry which at the same time brings into play the real and entire nature of man—asks not only about God but also about the possibility and the "practicality" of a genuine experience of God for the man of today, for whom God does not "happen" in the world. This theology, which inquires about God and yet may not deny the classical distinction between a metaphysical recognition of God and the theology of revelation about God, but must invade it and bring it to new unity, —this theology must take most seriously the quandary of contemporary man and his experience (no matter how badly misinterpreted) of the "death of God." It must identify with this experience. It may not merely prove from the contingency of the ultimate existent and from a formal transcendence of the spirit, that with the assumed experience of this contingency and transcendence the existence of God is implied. Theology must ask more precisely where and how contemporary man can experience the existence of God to such an extent that he can genuinely and voluntarily make it a real factor in his life; and theology must so do this that it does not give the hopeless impression that one ought to say nothing about something about which ultimately nothing can be said, and thereby situate the "unsaid God" somewhere within the range of option between a bitter and absurd existence and the blind courage of action.

There is also the question of Christ, whose evolutionary "*Weltanschauung*" stands on the horizon of salvation history and from the very beginning embraces all humanity, and which, furthermore, allows Christ to be seen as truly the summit of all salvation and revelation history. This conceptualization must be the basis for the new Christology, and this new Christology must avoid any undertone which might sound mythological to the modern ear; its method must retread the path of the earliest Christology (that is, the Christology *before* St. Paul and St. John) from the historical Jesus to the Christ of faith.

Again, there is the question of anthropology, a science which shows the man of today who and what he really is, how his existence entails more than the *animal rationale* of an abstract metaphysic. A Christian anthropology must be developed which will comprehend the original unity of nature and grace, and not confine that which we call Christian grace to a realm beyond concrete existence. It must be an anthropology which will not simply leave to moral theology or pious literature the questions of interpersonal communication, of love, of the experience of the absurd, of death.

Finally, there is the question of all that could go under the heading of dogmatic eschatology. Here there is lacking a real hermeneutics of eschatological declarations: there must be a far more radical consideration of the state of individual and collective eschatology if the proclamation of the last things is to be convincing today. The keynote of the existence of contemporary man is not of the kind which would allow him easily to revert to the Old Testament attitude towards the "beyond." The hope and the postulate of eternal individual life are no longer self-evident verities from which one might proceed as from a point of departure (as one could, perhaps, have done in the rationalistic age of the Enlightenment), but they are, rather, attitudes into which the man of today and tomorrow must be cautiously re-initiated. The Christian eschatology is not yet sufficiently confronted with the secular-utopian eschatology of the now-beginning era of one humanity, of the hominisation of the environment and man's singular control of his own destiny. A theology of hope is yet to be developed from Scholastic theology's dry account of the theological virtue of hope. There does not yet exist a theological ontology of hope, a theology which shows that man is essentially the hoping being, whose hope has an originality not adequately attributable to the recognition of the possible and the becomingness of a *be*-ing. Only such a theology of hope could be truly commensurate with the Marxist concept of man. The dialogue called for by the *Pastoral Constitution on the Church in the Modern World* has yet to take place. In a word, the overriding proposition which the Council prescribed for the theology of tomorrow is not a proposition which the Council itself treated (that is, if we ignore for a moment the allusions to it in the *Pastoral Constitution on the Church in the Modern World*), namely, that proposition regarding the last "foundations" of the Christian message on which the whole hierarchically structured edifice of Catholic dogmatics rests, the very last thing, which implies at once the final agony and the most sublime vocation of man. *This* is what today's theology must consider if it would be a theology worthy of the Council, and it must consider

96

it with a faith which is vulnerable, which makes clear what was heretofore incomprehensible, with a faith which renders incomprehensible what was heretofore clear.

It would be good, moreover, if theology could find a way of telling man briefly—and yet comprehensibly—just what it is that Christianity proclaims and mediates. This does not mean that there is a need to replace or supersede the Apostles' Creed. But very little effort is made to avoid the situation where contemporary man, for all the variegated theology and preaching, can no longer see the forest for the trees, and thus never attain to the fundamentals of the faith. Moreover, on the other hand, theology must present these fundamentals to modern man within the framework of a "formula" which will dynamically impel him to the fullness of faith, for the fundamentals of the faith are also structured within the hierarchy of truths (see Article 11 of the *Decree on Ecumenism*), and it is only in the light of this hierarchy that the complicated structure of Christian doctrine becomes comprehensible and credible. There are already such creedal formulas (and they need not necessarily be composed of one or a few sentences only): 1 Cor. 15, 3–5, and 1 Thess. 1, 9–10, are probably the first authoritative ones in scriptural tradition; the *Decree on the Church's Missionary Activity* contains the most recent one (Article 13). But much remains to be done in this direction. One must especially beware of a too quick acceptance of the formula of the "incarnation of the Word" as comprehensible and credible, since with no further clarification it easily becomes so misunderstood or so truncated that it is almost instinctively rejected as myth. One must never imagine that if one says "God," the word is immediately understood to mean what it *really* means.

It appears to me that it is only through the undertaking of these and similar tasks by systematic theology that a genuine and promising comprehension of ecumenical theology can be gained. Certainly, there must be a direct ecumenical theology, a theology of dialogue and controversy, which will treat of the doctrinal differences between the Christian professions, which will attempt to clear up misunderstandings, which will slowly learn to translate reciprocally the various language of these separate theologies. It must be a theology of controversy which will strive after unity, and not always after ever more subtle justifications for the split in the Church.

Surely, far more has been accomplished, and successfully, in this area in the past few decades than ever before. But needless to say, much more can and must be done.

It must also be clearly emphasized that we have much to learn not only from Protestant exegesis and biblical theology, but also from Protestant systematic theology. This task implies more than an initial searching out, in the themes of traditional controversial theology, the real import of the fathers of Protestantism, of their confessions of faith and their theologies today, in all their nuances. It means more than that we must overcome the often alarming simplification (and distortion) of their doctrines as they are all too often presented in our textbooks. (Of course, the same is true, all things being equal, of the Protestant understanding of Catholic doctrine.) Over and above such a study, there is also the need to investigate the vast body of questions and essays in Protestant theology which, though not directly and explicitly of a theologically controversial nature, are of supreme importance for the ecclesiology of both Churches.

The relationship between word and sacrament, or between the institution and the occurrence of grace, or questions relating to theological hermeneutics (to list only three examples), are not necessarily divisive themes in controversial theology. Rather, they are matters for common effort, matters in which Catholic theology has a great deal to learn from Protestant theology, matters in which the lines of interpretation at times cut across the boundaries of the various confessions. In short, our future theology must come to learn from Protestant systematic theology. From now on, our textbooks must no longer bring up the topic of Protestant theology at that point where it is necessary to report on the *adversarii* and their *errores*. These are very important, of course, and must be emphasized. But if ecumenism's only chance for a unified Christendom lies in the march towards a Church of the future (even the Catholic may say this, who believes in the lasting obligation of the Church's definitive dogma, and is convinced that the true Church of Christ subsists in the Roman Catholic Church), then this is all the more true of ecumenical *theology*. The different Churches and Christian communities will find a common language and a common creed only to the extent that they cease speak-

99

ing primarily of their doctrinal differences, and instead begin to coöperate in trying to master the new language of the future, in which the Gospel of Christ will be preached to the man of tomorrow in words which he can understand. (We might add parenthetically that this Gospel cannot be preached in the simplified abridgement, say, of Bishop John Robinson.)

The Christian theology for today's heathen is also the best ecumenical theology. Of course, efforts are still being made on both sides in this direction, but they are still insufficient quantitatively and qualitatively, especially on the Catholic side. Those thousands of volumes on atheism do not exist which should exist (if for no other reason than to balance the nearly countless number of volumes on Mariology which have been written). Assuming this conclusion to be correct, a similar observation may well be made regarding Protestant theology. It is that Protestant orthodox theology—which of all the Protestant theologies is closest to Catholic theology—is especially in danger of remaining a theology for an ever diminishing circle of the devout faithful; it is in danger of neglecting to develop a theology of tomorrow for the heathen, with whom we will live in the diaspora of tomorrow. But if such a theology of tomorrow is initiated by both sides, this will be the most important and the most encouraging aspect of an ecumenical theology. Is it not possible, for example, that if Protestant theology is able to present the doctrine of justification in a way which is truly credible to modern man (and we certainly recognize the burden and difficulty of this task), —is it not possible, then, that Catholic theology may also affirm the truth of this doctrine, and share it with Protestant theology? If we Catholics can learn to see more clearly, in a theology participating in the dialogue with the man of today, that the question of morality is in the final analysis still the question of God, of his grace, and of faith, —is it not then possible that the Protestant can come to understand that even among us Catholics the theology of self-justification is not sovereign, but that even for us, faith can be the key word for our relationship with God?

When on both sides there eventually prevails the determined effort not to justify historically, sociologically, psychologically, and ethnically determined differences and divisions in the Churches, but earnestly to seek a mutually acceptable creed, only then may we hope, *contra spem in spem,* for a unity in the Church which embraces all those who without reserve confess Jesus Christ as Lord. (This creed, in spite of perhaps lasting and profound differences between the theologies, will be sufficient for a unity of the Church in baptism and the Eucharist, and for a social unity as it is required by the will of Christ. Moreover, this unity will not be forthcoming until the Catholic Church exacts nothing more from her separated brethren than what her true dogma and her *jus divinum* require—and a definite resolution of this point is yet to be made.)

We must speak also of another theology and its future task, namely, practical theology, or as it is commonly known, pastoral theology. Now, after a Council which purported to be itself pastoral; after a Council in which the Church explicitly reflected on the newness of the future into which she proceeds; after a Council which treated of the episcopal college, the episcopal office, the episcopal conferences, the responsibility of the whole Church in the missions, and of each local Church for the whole Church, —after such a Council, pastoral theology can no longer content itself with being a storehouse of pious advice to the simple pastor of souls for the holy and effective fulfillment of his ministry.

Today practical theology must consider the total realization of the Church, and this with the help of theological reflexion on the present state of the Church. If the Council happened to draw up a separate *Pastoral Constitution on the Church in the Modern World,* then surely this is a theme for theology; it is a theme which must be explored in all its details, made explicit, subjected to theological method. For where else can the theme "the Church in the modern world" become explicit, taking into account all related matters, except in pastoral theology? This becomes clear from the very title of this constitution, and from the emphasis in the *Decree on Priestly Formation* on the necessity for a distinct discipline of pastoral theology, and the Council's desire that this discipline permeate and fecundate all other disciplines of theology as well.

Canon Law cannot bring this about. And this is so not only because Canon Law is oriented more towards the history and interpretation of existing law than to the question of *lege ferenda,* but also and above all because the total realization of the Church does not coincide with the observance of explicitly formulated legal norms—neither of those which exist, nor of those which ought to exist. In an age of cybernetics, of social super-organizations, certain questions can no longer be entrusted paternalistically merely to the wisdom, the circumspection, and the experience of ecclesiastical leaders—questions, for example, as to how the Church as a whole ought to live and act; how the central Roman authority ought to be structured; how a diocese ought to be organized; how the broad "politics" of spirit and culture ought to be influenced. Surely the Church leaders have the final decision in such matters, but the contemplation and study preparatory to all questions relating to the actual self-realization of the Church are today acutely in need of scientific method and systematic carrying through. A practical theology is needed which will take into account all that and more than what we have here only touched upon. The pastoral Council has called for a new pastoral theology which will be considerably enlarged in scope, and more attentive to method—a pastoral theology which, within the permanent structure of an ecclesiology of the immutability of the Church, and by means of a theologically enlightened view of the *status quo,* will seek to answer at least approximately the imperative needs of the man of today and tomorrow. In the light of a pastoral theology so understood,

that is, as a scientific theology with its own formal object
and its own method, we can surely say that everything in
this connection still remains to be done.

The Council's challenge to theology is very great, probably
greater than the Council Fathers themselves realized. Moreover, the renewal in theology, its *aggiornamento,* is (to
make a final point) to be promoted by the official Church.
It is to be promoted not only by means of the regional conferences of bishops meeting at the injunction of the Council
in order to determine and allow a new *ratio studiorum* for
the formation of priests. It is to be promoted not only in
that the bishops will liberally and courageously release sufficient priests for scientific endeavor, in spite of the so-called
(though partly real) scarcity of priests. It is to be promoted
not only in that the bishops will foster the training of lay
theologians, even beyond the need to supply a sufficient
number of religion teachers, and provide the lay theologian
with tasks and possibilities within the range of actual theological science—for teaching and ministry in the Church
need not always be identical. (For example, why should
there be no lay professors in Catholic theological faculties?
Is it possible, without betraying the spirit of the Council, to
deny the layman functions in the Church which are not
necessarily related to the priesthood?) It will be promoted
not only in that the local bishops, according to circumstances, will maintain contact with the theologians they met
in Rome—to the joyful surprise both of themselves and the
theologians—as useful for their purposes, and also as a bless-

ing for theology. The Church will promote theology not only in that the papal secretariats for ecumenism, for the non-Christian religions, and for modern atheism, can accomplish their task only through a renewed theology, and must therefore foster such a theology.

Since this world has become one of science, of intellectuals and professionals, the official Church can and must attend— even beyond the above mentioned ways—to the fostering of theological science. There is still room for considerable progress in the internationalization of Catholic theology. Why could there not be internationally approved and organized areas of specialization in theology (since no one can do everything), for the good of and with the participation of all Catholic theology? Could there not be collections (if on a more modest scale) throughout the Church for the benefit of Catholic theology, just as they are taken up for the Catholic missions? Could not the contact between ecclesiastical administration and ecclesiastical science be much closer—in fact, institutionally prescribed? Could not the Holy Office positively foster theology by assigning teams of theologians various "areas of investigation"? These theologians need not necessarily be stationed in Rome. (For example, in studying the *Constitution on the Sacred Liturgy,* one might doubt whether the 1957 decision of the Holy Office on concelebration might have been made as it was, had an international commission of experts in theology and liturgy first studied the problem.)

In short, should not theologians be organized to a greater

105

extent than is now customary? Such organization in other areas of scientific endeavor has become quite commonplace, and its benefits are quite well known to all.

Programs and institutions, however, cannot replace the creative man, and certainly least of all in theology. For theology will always remain the gift of the Spirit to the Church. But even so, the Spirit will always summon theology, and strengthen it, and help it to comprehend the yearnings and the needs of the time. There must be theology, for the "word of the Lord must speed on and triumph" (2 Thess. 3, 1). If theology trusts in the grace of God, and if it is truly informed of its mission in the world of tomorrow, then it will be good theology, and it will accomplish that which the Council empowered it to do.